Stone Painting
for Kids

Stone Painting for Kids

Designs to Spark Your Creativity

F. Sehnaz Bac

Dover Publications, Inc.
Mineola, New York

Bibliographical Note

Stone Painting for Kids is a new work, first published by
Dover Publications, Inc., in 2018.

Library of Congress Cataloging-in-Publication Data

Names: Bac, F. Sehnaz, author.
Title: Stone painting for kids / F. Sehnaz Bac. 7464383
Description: Mineola, New York : Dover Publications, 2018.
Identifiers: LCCN 2017037481| ISBN 9780486819037 (paperback) | ISBN 0486819035
Subjects: LCSH: Stone painting—Technique—Juvenile literature. | BISAC:
    JUVENILE NONFICTION / Activity Books. | JUVENILE NONFICTION / Art /
    Painting. | JUVENILE NONFICTION / Art / Techniques. | CRAFTS & HOBBIES /
    Crafts for Children.
Classification: LCC TT370 .B34 2018 | DDC 745.7/23—dc23
LC record available at https://lccn.loc.gov/2017037481

Manufactured in the United States by LSC Communications
81903501   2018
www.doverpublications.com

This book is dedicated to my daughters,
Ayse and Zeynep Meric, and
my husband, Artabano Forcellese,
for their patience and support.

Contents

Bonus!

67

Stone Painting

A TOTALLY FUN THING TO DO!

Painting on stones and pebbles will give you moments of fun, tranquility, and relaxation. It will teach you to exercise concentration as well as creativity. From the instant you first pick up a stone when walking in nature, until you give away your creation to a parent or friend, decorate your room with it or play with it, you will enjoy this increasingly popular hobby.

In *Stone Painting for Kids,* you will find plenty of ideas, from simple, basic shapes to more detailed designs. All of them will spark your own imagination for new designs and may even come from inspiration of your daily life: school, home, pets, games, and more. The unique shape of each stone will be the base that guides you in creating unique works. And thanks to the step-by-step instructions, you will master the techniques in no time, using inexpensive materials that are easily found in stationery and craft shops.

You can also draw and paint variations of the designs in this book, where you will find plenty of ideas to tweak to your own taste. The stylized designs I made are meant to help you apply your creativity and guide you into making your unique painted stones.

Don't worry about your artistic level! One of the goals of this book is to help you achieve your own way of painting while having fun with family and friends.

You will feel proud to decorate your home with your stone paintings and to be able to give them to your loved ones.

PICKING THE PERFECT STONES

A day with family and friends by the sea, river, or lake is a fun and healthy way to spend time together. It also offers you an incredible variety of stones to pick from. Water makes them smooth and round and ready to be used for your stone painting project. Their unusual shapes and beauty may give you the inspiration for new designs you had not thought of before.

It's best to choose smooth, flat stones and pebbles in different shapes and sizes. But you can collect irregular and rough ones if you like the shape. Don't forget to ask an adult if there is a ban on removing any natural objects from the area you are visiting.

If you are unable to visit any places with stones, no problem! Craft stores and garden supply stores offer a variety of stones.

PREPARING THE STONES

Before you start stone painting, the rocks need to be cleaned. Place them in a container full of water, and wash them with a soft brush or toothbrush and some mild soap. Rinse them under running tap water, and place them in the sun for a whole day to dry thoroughly. When the stones are completely dry, you can start with your first project.

If you find that a stone is still rough, applying white acrylic paint by pressing the brush on it will help fill the pores. Also, if you like to paint on a colored background, you can cover the stone's surface with acrylic paint, and after it dries, you can draw your designs on the colored surface.

SUPPLIES

To sketch your designs on stones and pebbles, you will need pencils and sharpeners. Use a regular pencil to draw on lighter surfaces and a white pencil for darker ones. If you make a mistake, erase it.

Acrylic paints are easy to apply, their colors are rich and bright, and they are indelible and nonfading once they dry. Your stone paintings will pop! Acrylic paint can be found in glass jars, tubes, and plastic containers, and it is important to remember that it dries out very quickly. So be careful, and always close any container when not in use. If you want to mix colors on your palette, apply only small quantities. Also, it is always better to ventilate the area where you are working, so open up some windows and the door. You will need a water container (a jar or a plastic cup will work just fine), paper towels, and a palette (a plastic plate can be used) to work with. And it's always best to use an apron to protect your clothes. Water-based craft colors can be used as an alternative to acrylic paint.

You will need brushes too! Round-tip synthetic brushes are good for all projects, and flat ones are useful to paint the stone's surface. Testing different sizes and shapes will give you an idea about which brushes are easier and better to use. Never leave brushes in water; this will spoil their shape. They must be washed with clean water every time you finish painting.

Colored pens and paint pens are easy to use when you want to draw designs on pebbles, and the colors dry fast. Colored felt-tip pens and markers can be used on light-colored stones, such as white ones. Pens and markers work best on smooth surfaces. Do not press your colored pens too hard on the stone's surface; this will protect their tips for a long time. Paint pens are good for details and for coloring your designs. They work with a pump system: after you shake a pen, you have to press gently several times so the paint gets to the tip. Practice with a paint pen on a piece of paper and then use it on a stone. Ask a grown-up to help you the first time you use one.

Watercolors, crayons, and colored pencils also can be used for stone painting. Remember: the designs you create with these will not be permanent.

TECHNIQUES

Once you have your stones, pebbles, and supplies ready, you can start! Begin with simple projects, and with time and practice, you will become an expert stone painter.

Before you start to draw your design, choose between leaving the stone's surface natural or applying a colored base. However, nothing is permanent . . . or wrong. You can always change your mind!

First, sketch the design on paper to see how it will come out. Once you are happy with the result, outline it on your stone with pencil. You can easily erase any mistakes. When the design is complete, you can paint in the parts with acrylic paints and brushes, or paint pens, or colored pens. Make sure you paint over all pencil lines for a clean look. If you do not wish to wait ten to twenty minutes for the paint to dry, use a blow dryer, set to Warm. Be sure to have a grown-up help you with this!

I prefer to outline the designs with a black pen, which will make them look even better. But you can leave them out, if you wish.

Once the paint and outlines are applied, have fun adding details: lines, triangles, circles, dots, squares . . . whatever comes to mind! Mix tools and materials, depending on your taste and mood. The possibilities are endless. Just make sure to dry your stone for twenty-four hours.

Use acrylic transparent varnish (matte or glossy) to protect your stone paintings from dust, water, and scratches. The finish can be applied with a brush or sprayed on. Ask an adult to help you with this outside or in a well-ventilated area.

SHOW OFF YOUR PAINTED STONES!

Your stone paintings will make beautiful gifts for family, friends, classmates, and teachers. Birthdays and holidays, anniversaries, and other occasions will give you opportunities to make original, unique creations. Stone paintings also can be used to decorate your room and desk, as bookends or paperweights, as ornaments in gardens, flowerpots, paths, and fountains.

Pebbles can be glued to a magnet and placed on the refrigerator door, or you can attach them to cardboard or mount them on a wood panel to create funny, humorous designs and beautiful pictures for everyone to enjoy!

Stone Painting for Kids

Geometric Shapes

1 You will need flat stones. Shape is not important, so you can choose oval, round, or irregular-shaped ones. Here are six stones. Using a pencil, draw basic geometric shapes on them: a rectangle, a square, an oval, a circle, a triangle, and a hexagon.

2 Color your shapes. You can use acrylic, watercolor, or tempera paint. Some round brushes such as numbers 3 and 4 are good choices. You can use felt-tip pens or paint pens for this step too.

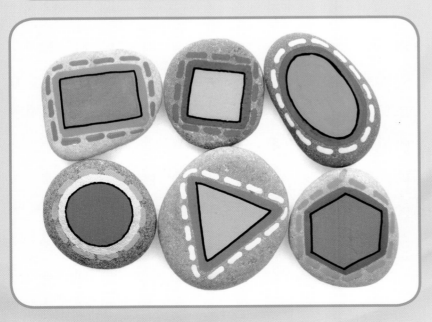

3 Now you can decorate your geometric shapes. First, draw a thin line around the edges of your shapes, using a black felt-tip pen. Then draw a thicker line around the black line, using a color that's different from the colors of your shapes. Next, draw dashed lines around the thick line with a third color. You will have the best-looking stones!

4 For another fun style, you can use masking tape. Wrap the tape to a portion of the stone (across the middle, for example). Make sure the tape is firmly pressed onto the surface. Paint one uncovered part of the stone with the color of your choice.

5 Paint the other uncovered part of the stone with a different color and wait for the paint to completely dry. Carefully remove the tape.

6 Repeat steps 4 and 5 for each section you wish to color. If you find some areas where paint leaks when the tape is pulled off, don't worry! You can paint over these parts with a brush or paint pen of the same color.

Try It!

You can leave your designs as they are or decorate them even more. Add new sections and decorations with a ruler and paint pens or brushes.

Numbers

1 Choose smooth, flat stones. This will make it easy for you to write numbers on them.

2 Write your numbers with large-tip paint pens, using different colors. Keep your numbers simple, or draw dots and small lines around them with different colors.

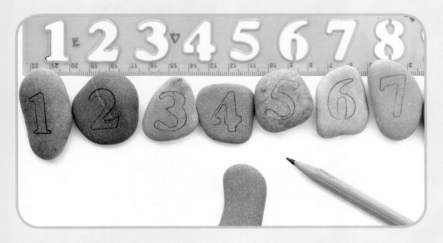

3 Another way to write numbers on your stones is to use number stencils. Place the stencil on the stone's surface and carefully trace the number with a pencil. If you make a mistake, you can erase it and try again.

4 Fill your numbers with the colors of your choice. Try to paint with care and stay inside the lines. I used black paint for the numbers, but you can try other colors for a different look.

Letters

A B C D E
F G H I J
K L M N O
P Q R S T
U V W X Y Z

1 Try to find flat stones with similar shapes to the alphabet's twenty-six letters.

2 Paint the surface of the stones with different colors. Acrylic paints have the brightest colors, but you can use tempera, poster paint, or watercolors.

3 When the stones are completely dry, draw the outline of your letters. For lighter background colors, use a pencil. For darker surface colors, use a white pencil.

4 Paint your letters with colors that go well with the background colors. You can use paint and brush or color paint pens. Outline your letters with black liner pens, felt-tip pens, or black paint pens. Now you're ready to spell words!

Hearts

1   You will need heart- and triangle-shaped stones. Use a pencil or paint to draw your heart on the stone's surface, or cover the stone with paint and then draw your heart.

2   When the paint dries, use paint pens to define the heart designs with bold, thick lines.

3   Add colorful bold lines with paint pens inside the original heart and outline them with a black pen. This helps the design pop! To add movement, draw some black lines inside a colored line.

4   If you want to add more details, decorate your red-painted stones with white lines, colored dots, and dashes using paint pens. For the green/purple/yellow heart, add a pink outline and some pink, white, and turquoise dots.

Faces

1 Find round or oval stones. Here are four different possibilities. One features a sketch that separates the hair from the pink-colored face. Another shows hair and facial features. A third is a simple stone with eyes and a mouth. And a fourth is a paint-covered stone.

2 In this step, you can begin to add other features and skin-tone colors to the faces. Draw your face design on the painted stone with a pencil.

3 Using paint pens, fill the hair sections with fun colors. You can even add spirals. Draw dots for noses, and color the eyes and mouths. You can use a black pen for the details and colored pens for the eyes and mouths. Try painting faces with different expressions. The possibilities are endless!

1 Here is another fun way to paint faces. First, find some round and oval stones of different sizes and paint them with bright colors.

2 After the paint is dry, add eyes, noses, and mouths, using large paint pens. You can make two big white dots for eyes, a pink dot for the nose, and a red or black line for the mouth.

3 Add an outline with a thin black pen for all the facial features. You can draw black dots for pupils or glue on googly eyes, as shown here.

Try It!

Googly eyes imitate eyeball movement. Decorate your painted stones with these plastic eyes by gluing them on for a cute and goofy effect.

Multipebble Flowers

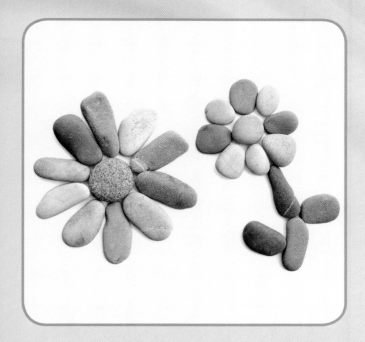

1 You will need round and oval or petal-shaped stones and pebbles. Form them into flowers on a flat surface. Use the pebbles for stems and leaves.

2 You can paint every petal a different color or make them all the same.

3 If you have a hard time painting the pebbles, stick double-sided tape on paper, peel off the other side of the tape, and adhere the pebbles to it. Now you can easily paint them. When one side dries, turn the pebbles over to paint the other side.

4 If you'd like to add extra details, paint droplike shapes on the petals and decorate the center pebble with dots and small lines. You can also put lines on the stems and leaves with a large-tip paint pen.

Mushrooms

1 Search for a stone with a triangular shape for the mushroom cap and a thin oval one for the stem.

2 Color the mushroom cap with red paint. Use light-brown paint for the stem. Let the paint dry completely.

3 To decorate the mushroom's cap, add big and small dots with a large white paint pen. Put some dark brown patches on the stem and green grass at the bottom.

4 Try different colors on your mushrooms. You can make them realistic or create imaginary ones with fantastical colors!

Dominoes

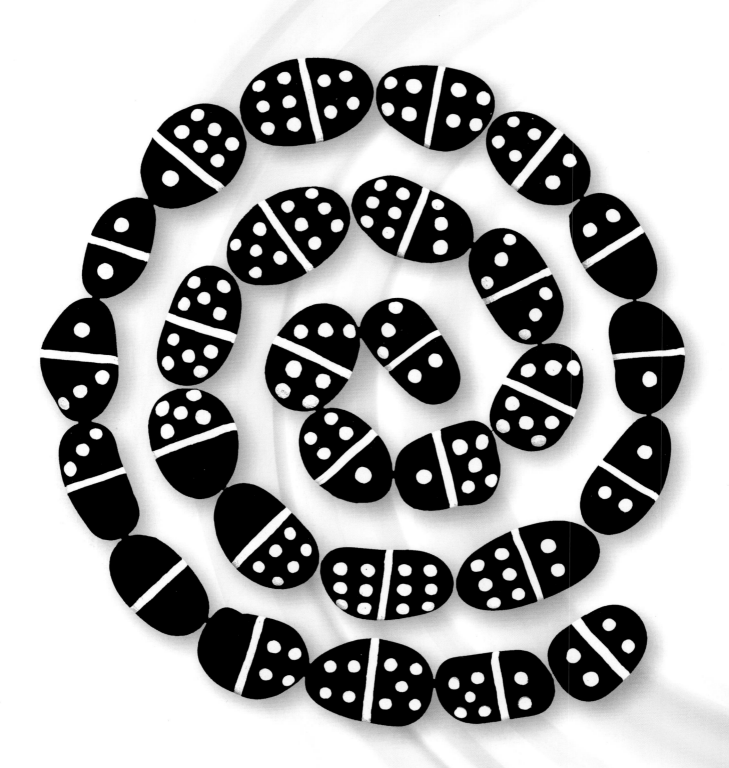

1 To create dominoes, you will need twenty-eight pebbles of similar size and shape. They don't need to be perfect rectangles. Flat oval pebbles will be fine.

2 Paint all your pebbles black. Refer to Multipebble Flowers Step 3 on page 17 to keep your pebbles from moving around.

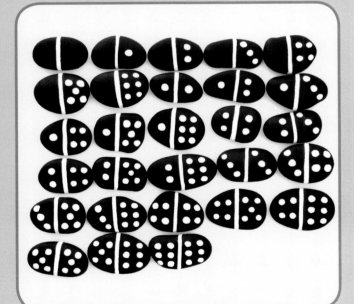

3 Using a white paint pen, draw a thick line in the middle of each pebble. Add the correct number of dots to each half. Look at a set of real dominoes to make sure you have all the correct combinations.

4 Cover your new domino stones with acrylic varnish to protect the paint and keep them looking new. With the help of a grown-up, you can use a liquid or spray version of transparent varnish.

Shellfish

1 Seashells, like stones, are very fine objects to paint. Collect different size shells, wash them with fresh water, and wait until they dry.

2 Now paint the shells with bright, bold colors to make a school of rainbow-colored fish. You can use acrylic paint, watercolors, tempera (poster paint), or gouache. Add two or three coats until the surface is covered. Make sure the paint dries completely between coats.

3 Look for oval or triangle-shaped pebbles for the fish tails and round pebbles for the eyes. Assemble your designs on a piece of cardboard.

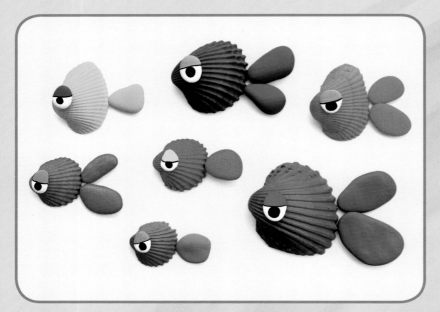

4 Paint the fish tails with the same color as the shells. For eyes, draw a line in the middle of the round pebbles with a black felt-tip pen. Paint the upper half with different colors and use white for the lower half. Next, put black dots in the lower part to complete the eyes.

5 Add some detail to the fish tails by painting the inner parts with a lighter shade of the same color.

6 Paint lines along the edge of the shells with contrasting colors. Now your fish are ready! You can mix or match the pieces. Also, create your own pictures by attaching them to a piece of cardboard with hot glue. Ask a grown-up for help.

Try It!

Your colorful school of fish could use an ocean or aquarium to swim in. Why not paint the cardboard background to create an underwater world?

Chess

1 Find thirty-two flat pebbles, sixteen of which should be smaller for the pawn pieces. Place them on a chessboard.

2 Choose two different colors to paint your pebbles, sixteen in one color and sixteen in another. Apply several coats of paint. Make sure the paint is dry before you start the next coat.

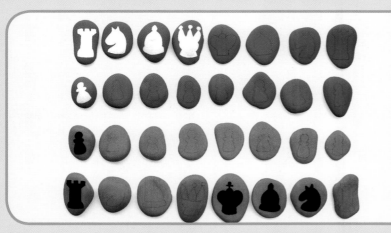

3 With a pencil, sketch the designs of the different chess pieces—pawns, knights, bishops, rooks, queens, and kings—on your stones. A grown-up can help you find pictures of them.

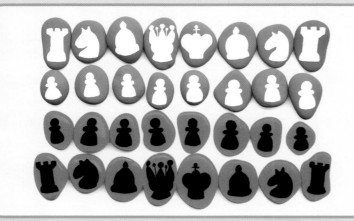

4 Paint the inside of your designs with colors that go well with the background color. For a little more detail, you can add lines and dots to your chess pieces. Remember to varnish your pebbles in order to protect them.

Multipebble
Rabbit

1 Search for an oval stone for the rabbit's body, a round pebble for the head, two thin oval pebbles for ears, and four oval or triangle-shaped pebbles for legs.

2 Color your stones and pebbles with acrylic paint. I used bright-pink, but you can choose your favorite color. What is it?

3 Paint a big oval inside the body stone with light-pink. Add similar patches to the ears and legs. With a white paint pen, draw the eyes and cheeks. Use a black pen to define the eyes, nose, mouth, whiskers, and toes.

4 Paint colorful dots on the body and ears. Highlight the lighter-colored parts of the body, ears, and legs with white. Your rabbit is now ready to hop, hop away!

Try It!

Make a bear, a giraffe, or a caterpillar. Attach the stones on cardboard or make a puzzle, mixing up the pieces and then matching the animals' correct parts.

Words

1 Find flat, smooth stones. They can be different shapes and sizes.

2 Paint the surface of the stones with fun colors, like lilac, green, pink, red, aqua, and yellow. Do not paint the edges, but leave them untouched.

3 What are your favorite words? Write them on the stones with large paint pens in colors that will be easily readable against the background.

4 Add big colorful dots to frame your words and smaller black dots inside the big ones. Your word stones are ready to decorate your bedroom or to give away as gifts.

believe

love

bloom

live

hope

happy

Try It!

Add different patterns—hearts, flowers, leaves, zigzags, or curves—on the painted parts of your stones.

Flowers

1 This project is different from Multipebble Flowers on pages 16–17. Instead of creating petals from different pebbles, paint all the petals on just one stone. Search for round stones for the flowers and thin oval ones for the stems and leaves.

2 Paint the stones with your favorite colors. Purple and red are mine. What are yours?

3 Sketch your flower designs on the stones. Use a regular pencil for light background colors and a white pencil or chalk for dark background colors. Draw some leaves on the stems.

4 Fill the petals and centers and the stems and leaves with bright colors, using paint and brush or paint pens. With a black felt-tip pen or paint pen, draw a line around all the parts of your designs.

Try It!

For even fancier flowers, add black or red lines and white, yellow, or black dots in the petals and leaves. What colors do you like?

Houses

1 Find flat rectangular- or triangular-shaped stones. You can paint the surfaces or leave them in their natural state.

2 Sketch the house designs on the stones with a pencil. Try different types of roofs, doors, and windows.

3 Now you can paint your designs with a variety of colors. Yellow windows make it look like the lights are on inside!

4 Using paint pens and a black fine-line pen, add curvy lines, big and small dots, semicircles, dashes, and more colors to your houses.

Shell Butterfly

1 You will need four seashells of two different sizes for the butterfly's wings, two thin oval pebbles for the body, and a round pebble for the head.

2 Starting at the outer edge of the shells and working your way in, paint thick, bold sections. Add colors to the body and head. I used red acrylic paint, but pick your favorite color!

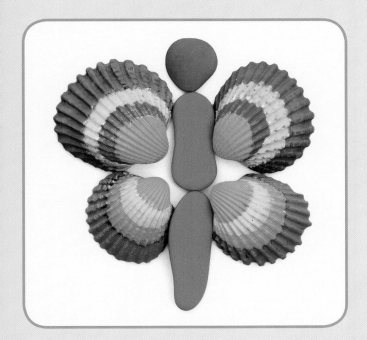

3 I created four bright sections on each shell. You may have to use several coats of paint because the shell's natural surface is rough and curvy and hard to cover. Make sure the paint dries after each coat.

4 Using a black paint pen and other colors, add lines, dashes, curves, dots, and facial features. Bend a piece of wire to get the right shape of the shell butterfly's antennae.

Vehicles

1 You will need a pencil and different-sized flat stones on which to sketch your boat and plane.

2 Now add colors to your designs. You can use paint pens or acrylic paint and brushes. I chose blue, white, red, and pink.

3 Draw a thin black line around the edges of your boat and plane. This will give them a sharp, defined look.

4 For more detail, add shapes and dots within the stripes of the boat's sail and along the hull. For the plane, make circles for the windows and paint stripes and dots to the wings and tail. Use a thin black pen to outline the cockpit window.

1 You will need a pencil and circular-shaped stones on which to sketch your car, truck, and bus.

2 Color your vehicles with paint pens or acrylic paint and brushes. You can choose realistic colors or have fun with more unusual ones. I used black for the tires.

3 Draw thin black lines around the edges and features of your vehicles. This will help distinguish the different parts of the car, truck, and bus.

4 You can add fun details like a small white circle inside the tires and tiny white dots for headlights. Other elements like zigzags can make your vehicles extra special.

1 You will need a pencil and flat, rectangular-shaped stones on which to sketch your train designs. I will draw an engine car at the front and passenger and freight cars behind it.

2 Paint the train cars with a variety of colors. Fill in the wheels with white paint. As you can see, this makes for a very bright train!

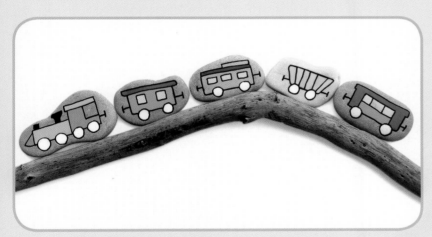

3 Draw a thin black line around the edges of the train cars, wheels, and windows. Now your train looks sharp.

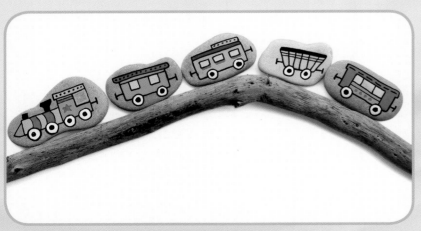

4 For more detail, add small dots or dashes on the roof of each train car, and stars, stripes, and circles on the body. Have fun with the colored pens or paint pens!

The Sky

1 You will need oval or round stones. Some irregular-shaped ones can be used as well. I chose three stones for a sun, a moon, and a cloud.

2 Paint all the surfaces with colors that match the subject: yellow for the sun, black for the moon's background, and blue for the cloud's sky.

3 For the sun, draw a circle in the center and triangle-shaped rays around it with a black paint pen. For the moon and the cloud, use a white paint pen to draw your designs.

4 Paint circles, lines, and dots to add more details to the sun, the moon, and the cloud.

Animals

1 Choose flat, smooth stones. It's easier if you first decide which animals you want to paint and then find stones to match their build. But don't worry! You can make any stone work.

2 Draw the animal designs on your stones with a pencil. That way, if you make a mistake, you can erase it. Here's a bear, a cat, a snake, a dog's face, and a paw.

3 Use your imagination to color the animals. After the paint has dried, draw thin black lines around all your designs.

4 Decorate your stones with simple details. Use lines and dots and triangles to make the animals come alive!

Tic-Tac-Toe

1 You will need at least nine round stones. Don't worry if they aren't the same size. Once you finish painting them, they will all look great!

2 Cover the stones with a layer of white acrylic paint. This helps to make the rough surfaces finer and smoother, and your designs will be more vivid.

3 Get your supplies ready. You will need a pencil, paint, and fine liner pens. Now you can create your designs on the stones. You'll find that there are different ways to do it.

4 With a pencil, draw a flower on the white background and paint the outside of the design red. You can also paint the surface red, and sketch a flower with a white pencil. Decide which way you like best.

5 Start to fill your flower petals with colors. Here I am going to use red stones with pink petals for one player and green stones with white petals for the other player.

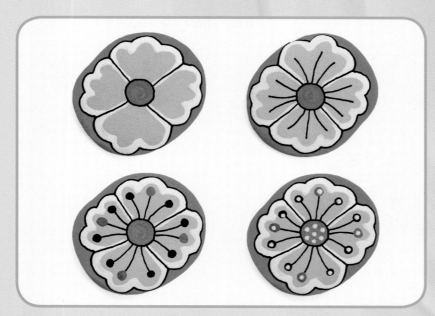

6 You can add different colors to the petals and a thin black line around the edges. Put black lines from the center out and end them with colored dots. Paint the other set of flowers the same way and then you'll be ready to play tic-tac-toe!

Try It!

Paint your tic-tac-toe stones with ladybug designs. Ask a grown-up to help you put transparent acrylic varnish on them for protection.

Multipebble Humans

1 Search for different-sized flat, round stones for heads, oval stones for bodies, and thin oval pebbles for arms and legs. Arrange the stones into human shapes and write the names of the body parts on the back of each one to easily reassemble them after painting.

2 Paint the heads, arms, and hands the same color, and the dresses, shoes, trousers, and socks different ones. Be sure to allow the paint enough time to dry before moving to the next step.

3 Now you can add faces. Choose hair colors and draw detailed strands using fine black lines. Be as creative as you want with the clothes! Use a jacket and tie for the man and colorful outfits with lines, dots, and curves for the child and the woman. Black lines and different color dots on the shoes are the perfect final touch!

Memory Game

1 You will need sixteen similar round or oval stones for the memory game.

2 Choose your favorite color and use it to paint all the stones. Be sure to cover the backs too. I used green.

3 Paint a circle with a lighter color on the stones, leaving a little bit of the background color around the edges. Bright-yellow is my choice. What's yours?

4 Sketch your designs in pairs, such as two fish, two ladybugs, two butterflies, and two owls. Draw the designs with a pencil. You can choose simpler forms like shapes, letters, and numbers. Make it easy for yourself!

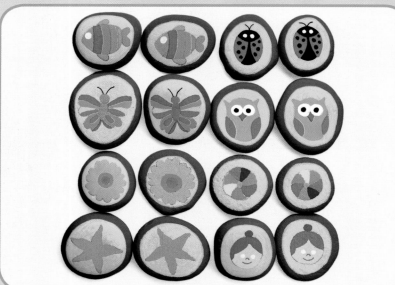

5 Paint your designs with bold, bright colors. Use paint pens or acrylic paint with brushes. Make sure the colors and patterns for each pair match!

6 For a sharper look, outline your designs in black. Details such as colorful lines and dots make for livelier pieces!

60

Try It!

Add a small design, such as a heart, on the back of the stones. That way, when they are turned over, they won't look plain.

Blackboard Stone

1 Choose a large, flat, smooth stone and paint it with black chalkboard paint. Wait at least six hours to make sure the paint is completely dry. The larger the stone, the more words and designs you will be able to make on the blackboard-style surface.

2 Using colored chalk markers or chalks, write whatever you want to say on the blackboard stone. Remember, you can easily erase things with a damp, soft cloth or with a blackboard eraser.

Washi Tape on Stones

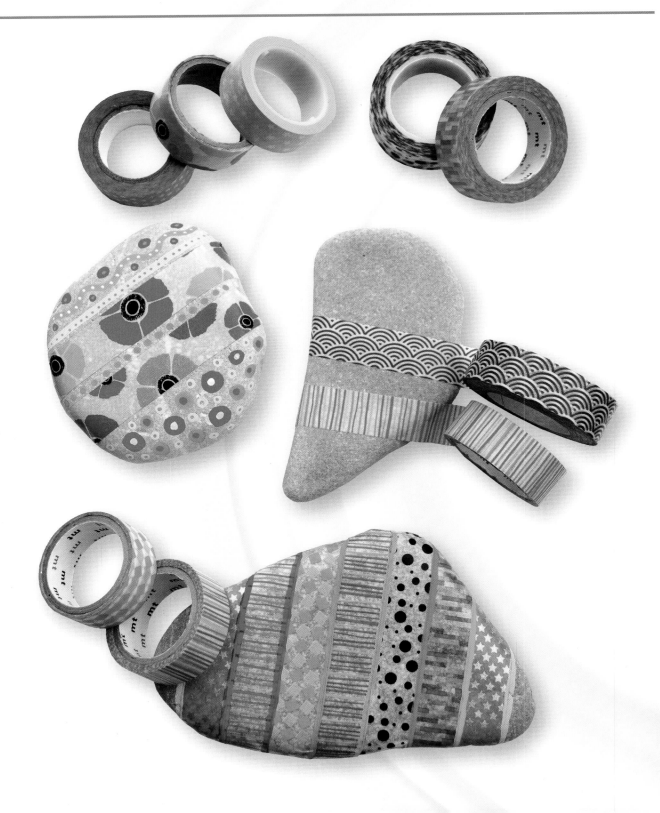

1 Search for large flat stones and choose colorful washi tape to work with. Adhere the tape side by side on each stone, leaving some of its natural surface showing on both ends.

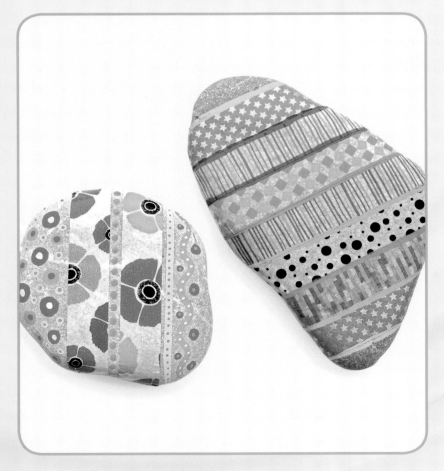

2 With paint pens, draw colorful lines between each strip of tape. You can also decorate the stone's natural surface with dots, curvy lines, and any pattern that appeals to you. This is a fun, easy project, and in the end you will have wild and crazy decorations for your bedroom or to give away as gifts!

STONE PLAY

Mathematics

Take your Numbers stone paintings from pages 6–7 and combine them with stones from other projects to create fun counting games. You may be the next Albert Einstein!

Scenes & Themes

A fun way to play with your stone paintings is to make a picture or an outdoor landscape. Place the different stone paintings together to create a theme such as the sky or forest animals.

Storytelling Stones

Tell a story with your stone paintings. Ask a grown-up or a friend to choose stones from your different collections and create a story, using all the designs. What tales can you make up?

Spelling Game

Practice spelling the names of the objects you painted on the stones.
In no time, you will be a spelling bee champ!

About the Author

F. Sehnaz Bac is from Istanbul, Turkey, and studied archaeology at Ege University. She has a master's degree in restoration and conservation from the Faculty of Architecture. For the past two decades, she has worked at excavation sites as an archaeologist and draftsperson. Her detailed technical drawings at these sites have informed her imaginative stone designs, which are inspired by nature and rendered brightly in watercolor, acrylic, ink, and marker pens.

Sehnaz displays her painted stones at www.facebook.com/isassidelladriatico and sells them at www.etsy.com/shop/isassidelladriatico.

4-19